Editor
Gisela Lee, M.A.

Managing Editor
Karen J. Goldfluss, M.S. Ed.

Editor-in-Chief
Sharon Coan, M.S. Ed.

Cover Artist
Brenda DiAntonis

Art Manager
Kevin Barnes

Imaging
Temo Parra

Product Manager
Phil Garcia

Publishers
Rachelle Cracchiolo, M.S. Ed.
Mary Dupuy Smith, M.S. Ed.

Mastering Word Problems
Grades 4–6

Author

Susan Anderson Mauck

Teacher Created Materials, Inc.
6421 Industry Way
Westminster, CA 92683
www.teachercreated.com
ISBN-0-7439-3357-5
©2004 Teacher Created Materials, Inc.
Made in U.S.A.

Table of Contents

Introduction

Teachers need to provide their students with opportunities to practice their math skills in real-life situations. Many states mandate tests that contain questions that require students to understand the language of math and to apply the skills they have developed to answer the questions. This resource book was created to meet that need. It can be used with students in fourth through sixth grade.

The practice pages are divided into four sections. The first section provides an opportunity for teachers and students to solve the problems together. These are referred to as "Whole-Class" sheets. The second section contains "Independent Practice Cards." Students may work on these cards with partners and when they are completed, they bring them up to get immediate feedback. The third section contains individual "Practice Sheets" for use in the classroom. Students can seek help from other classmates while solving the problems on these practice sheets. The fourth section contains worksheets to assign as homework. The homework pages allow the students opportunities to practice the skill of problem solving without the support of classmates and the teacher. Some students will need more support at home so included in this resource is a letter to the parents explaining the purpose of this type of math assignment and suggestions for helping their child.

Finally, there are tests you can administer to assess a student's mastery and use of some of the problem-solving methods they have learned throughout the book. Students have been encouraged to work with others to solve the problems, but it is important to measure how well they can solve problems on their own. Students should be reminded to do their own work so that the test serves as an accurate measurement of each student's ability to tackle this type of question. A range of levels for the assessment tests has been provided in this section.

Problem-Solving Strategies

Most intermediate students have already been taught a variety of strategies for solving problems. These strategies might include up to 12 standard strategies a student could use when confronted with a problem. These strategies usually include using objects, working backward, drawing a picture, acting out the problem, drawing diagrams, using number sentences, and making a table. Students are often overwhelmed by a list of strategies such as this. One way to simplify these strategies is to tell students to refer to all these strategies as "putting ideas on paper." The meaning of this phrase can be explained to the students as "putting down something on paper that will help you in your thinking." During the guided practice, you can demonstrate what you mean by "putting your ideas on paper." This simple language makes sense to children.

Often students do not understand a problem when they first read it. They need to take some time to understand what they have to do. Often they will understand better if they read the problem a second time. If that doesn't work, they can try to read the problem out loud. Next, they should put down on paper something that will help them with their thinking. It could be a picture of what they already know. It may be numbers and words that represent what they already know, whatever makes sense to them and that works with the given problem. They can read the problem again, out loud or silently. They need to be persistent. Make a poster of the following steps to remind students of what they should do when trying to solve math problems:

Problem-Solving Steps

- Read and Understand the Problem.
- Make a Plan.
- Solve the Problem.
- Check to Be Sure Your Answer Makes Sense.

Reproduce and distribute page 6. Read and discuss the information. Model a problem-solving situation using the Four-Step Plan.

Establishing a Successful Classroom Climate

This is important that teachers create a positive, supportive climate in their classrooms. Students need time to grapple with the problems and seek solutions. They need to feel safe to make mistakes. The emphasis should be on working on the problems, not in getting the right answers. It is important that the teacher place more value on effort and perserverence than on speed.

Students should realize that it is normal to feel some frustration when solving problems. They need to persevere when they feel like giving up. If their frustration is too great, they should take some time out to work on another problem or take a break. The teacher's role is to help students realize that frustration is normal and to step in if a student is too discouraged.

Students Support Each Other

Students should be encouraged to help each other with their thinking, especially during the beginning stages of problem solving. Students can be grouped into teams of three or work with partners. Teams or partners can be selected at random, or the teacher can determine the groups to meet individual needs. It is often helpful to pair a more capable student with a less capable one. At the beginning of the school year, each student can be paired with a "work partner" for various learning activities. In this way a positive working relationship with another student can already be in place before students tackle the problem-solving activities.

When working with partners, students need to understand that they do not help someone by giving them the answers. It is important that all students working together understand how they arrived at the solutions. Remind them often that the process is more important that just getting the correct answers.

Make Your Expectations Clear

Post your expectations during any problem solving activity to remind students of your expectations. Keep them simple to be most effective. An example of these might be the followimg:

> 1. Stay on task.
>
> 2. Help each other.
>
> 3. Don't give up!

Importance of Showing Your Work

Sometimes there may be more than one possible solution to a problem. Encourage students to show their work. Tell them that showing their work helps the person who is grading their papers know what they were thinking. Students are reminded of this in the directions for the cards, practice pages, and tests.

When students have answered a problem incorrectly, look for parts of their work that show correct thinking. Sometimes a student will do everything correctly but make a simple error in computation. If students arrive at a wrong answer, give partial credit if they have shown evidence of correct thinking.

The Teacher's Role

Teachers need to present themselves as active problem solvers, as people who don't always know the answers but work hard to figure them out. Students need to see that the teacher values the problem-solving process rather than merely getting the answers right. Teachers need to model the behavior they want to see in their students.

It is important for the teacher to move about the room during problem-solving sessions. It is his or her job to listen to the ideas being shared between partners or in groups. The teacher should offer assistance when needed but not interrupt a group that is working well.

There are generally two types of problems that occur when students are solving problems in groups. Sometimes the students have difficulty understanding the problem. They may be at a dead end or pursuing a wrong line of thought. If they're unable to progress, the teacher can help by having a student reread the question out loud. Ask someone to explain what he or she thinks the question is asking. Often merely restating the question can help a student understand.

Sometimes the difficulty lies in the group. The teacher can join a group for a short time to help them focus. They may need clarification about the steps they should take to solve the problem. Avoid telling students what they should do; rather, ask questions to help them become aware of what they might try.

Groups also may have problems if one person takes over and ignores the others' ideas. It is the teacher's role to remind students that their goal is to work together to solve the problems, that everyone in the group needs to understand how a problem was solved. Remember, if your students are to be successful problem solvers, you need to be actively involved. Sitting at a desk grading papers while students are working is not good teaching practice.

Summing Up

After a problem-solving session, it is a good idea to have students report about the process. They can share their ideas about solving particular problems. This can help others see the variety of ways to approach a problem.

Provide opportunities for students to share the feelings they had during the process. A student who is frustrated will be reassured to hear that others felt similarly. It is also beneficial to discuss how individuals dealt with their frustration. Many students really enjoy solving the problems and can share the feelings of excitement and satisfaction they felt as they figured out the solutions. A student who is not already experiencing this kind of success can benefit from hearing how others feel.

Getting Started

Here is some information about how to use a multiple-step approach to solving word problems.

Four-Step Plan

1. **Read and Understand the Problem.**

   Trying to solve a problem without understanding it would be like jumping into the deep end of a pool without knowing how to swim. Ask yourself these questions to help understand the problem better:

   - Why is this problem important?
   - What do I need to find out?
   - What information do I know?
   - Do I have all the information I need to solve it?

2. **Make a Plan.**

   Consider planning your swimming lesson. After you decide what you need to find out, decide how to go about discovering the answer. Some valuable problem-solving strategies include the following:

   — acting it out   — working backward
   — drawing a picture   — making a list
   — looking for a pattern   — making a table or chart
   — guessing and checking   — using logical reasoning

3. **Solve the Problem.**

   Now you can jump into the pool and put those swimming lessons to use. Use the strategy you think best to solve the problem. Then find the answer.

4. **Check to Be Sure Your Answer Makes Sense.**

   If you've applied your lessons correctly, you are swimming by now. Check your answer. Does it make sense? Check to make sure your answer is not unreasonable. Estimation is an important skill. If you expected the answer to be about 400 and you come up with 2,000, chances are you did something wrong.

   Also, be sure you answered the question that was asked. If a problem asks you to identify the fruit you are most likely to randomly select from a bowl, the answer isn't 32 or 5/9, it's perhaps "an apple" or "a banana."

   Refer to this four-step plan with each word problem you encounter in this book. If you do, you'll be ready to swim through the challenge of solving word problems without any assistance!

Whole-Class Practice

Help students build their problem-solving skills by solving some problems as a whole class. You can make a transparency copy of the problems on the "Whole-Class Practice" sheets or write them on the board. It is best not to hand the problems out to students on paper at this point. Students who are skilled at problem solving and enjoy it will have the problems solved before you've had a chance to even begin your instruction. This is a good time to explain why partial credit is given when students get an answer wrong but have shown correct thinking in their work.

If you are using an overhead projector, cover all but the directions to begin your lesson. Discuss the importance of showing your work, then checking your math and making sure you have answered the question before starting your whole-class. Then model this in your lesson.

Display the "Four-Step Plan" Poster and guide students through the process as you solve the problems together. In this way, students are set up for success as you model the steps.

Whole-Class Practice 1

Show your work. Let the person who is checking your paper know what you were thinking as you solved the problems. Read each problem carefully. When you are done solving each problem, check your math and make sure you answered the question.

1. In the first week it is open, a toy store sells 45 baseballs. In its second week, the store sells 20 baseballs more than it sold in the first week. How many baseballs did the toy store sell in the two weeks?

2. James collects baseball cards. He recently added two dozen cards to his collection. If James had 345 cards in his collection before, how many does he currently have?

Whole-Class Practice 2

Show your work. Let the person who is grading your paper know what you were thinking as you solved the problems. Read each problem carefully. When you are done solving each problem, check your math and make sure you have answered the question.

1. The Amazon River is 6,437 km long. The Nile River is 234 km longer than the Amazon. The Mississippi River is 700 km shorter than the Nile River. How long is each of the rivers?

2. Sally has $20 to spend at the store. She buys a notebook that costs $2.99, a stuffed animal that costs $5.99, and a game that costs $5.79. (Prices include tax.) What change should she receive if she pays with a $20 bill?

Whole-Class Practice 3

Show your work. Let the person who is grading your paper know what you were thinking as you solved the problems. Read each problem carefully. When you are done solving each problem, check your math and make sure you answered the question.

1. George had 40 cookies. He divided the cookies equally into five boxes. Then he gave one of the boxes to a friend. How many cookies did George have left?

2. Jan and Cathy had six cookies each. Jenny had five cookies, and Tina had three cookies. They put all of the cookies in one big pile. Then they divided them into equal piles and each girl took a pile. How many cookies did each girl get?

Whole-Class Practice 4

Show your work. Let the person who is grading your paper know what you were thinking as you solved the problems. Read each problem carefully. When you are done solving each problem, check your math and make sure you answered the question.

1. A local service organization wanted to raise money for a school and encourage recycling. They offered 10¢ for each aluminum can the fourth grade classes could collect in the month of March. The graph shows how many cans each class collected.   How much money did Mrs. Falk's class earn for the school?

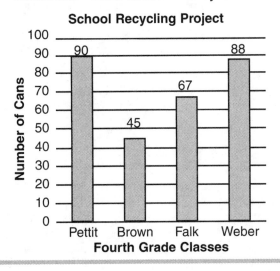

2. A group of 24 students, one teacher, and five parents took several cars to Highbanks Metro Park. If each car held five people how many cars did they take?

Whole-Class Practice 5

Show your work. Let the person who is grading your paper know what you were thinking as you solved the problems. Read each problem carefully. When you are done solving each problem, check your math and make sure you answered the question.

1. You reach into a bag that contains five sharpened pencils and 10 unsharpened pencils. Without looking, you reach in and pull out an unsharpened pencil. Predict the kind of pencil you are likely to get the second time you reach into the bag. Explain your answer.

2. The local theater is divided into three sections. Each section has a different number of seats. The chart shows how many seats each section holds. For the first showing of a movie, all the seats were filled, except for 50 empty seats. How many people were sitting in the theater?

Theater Section	Number of Seats
front section	100
back section	120
balcony	80

Whole-Class Practice 6

Show your work. Let the person who is grading your paper know what you were thinking as you solved the problems. Read each problem carefully. When you are done solving each problem, check your math and make sure you answered the question.

1. Danny bought four packs of paper that cost $2.79 each. (Price includes tax.) He paid for them with a $20 bill. What was his change?

2. Mrs. Hilton, the principal, needs to buy Popsicles™ for all the students in her school. There are 82 students in the 1st grade, 77 students in the 2nd grade, 67 students in the 3rd grade, 62 students in the 4th grade, and 74 students in the 5th grade. Show how Mrs. Hilton could use front-end estimation to decide how many Popsicles she should buy.

Whole-Class Practice 7

Show your work. Let the person who is grading your paper know what you were thinking as you solved the problems. Read each problem carefully. When you are done solving each problem, check your math and make sure you answered the question.

1. Mr. Blain was grouping the students in his school into basketball teams. There were 52 students who wanted to participate. He wanted no more than four students on each team. How many teams would he have?

2. Marla works at a jewelry store. Her hourly wage is $5.50. You want to find out how much money Marla is paid each week. What piece of information do you need to help you find out?

   A. The number of hours she works on weekdays.
   B. The number of hours she works each week.
   C. The number of days she works each week.

Whole-Class Practice 8

Show your work. Let the person who is grading your paper know what you were thinking as you solved the problems. Read each problem carefully. When you are done solving each problem, check your math and make sure you answered the question.

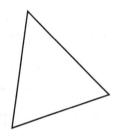 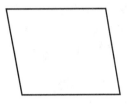  

1. Read the sentences. Circle each sentence that tells how all the figures above are alike.

   - They are polygons.
   - They are closed figures.
   - They have parallel sides.
   - They are three dimensional.
   - They have curved sides.
   - They have at least one right angle.

2. Make the smallest sum possible with these digits: 3, 5, 9, 2. Put each of these digits in one of the boxes below to make 2 two-digit numbers.

   Try to get the smallest sum you can.

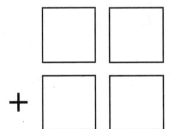

Whole-Class Practice 9

Show your work. Let the person who is grading your paper know what you were thinking as you solved the problems. Read each problem carefully. When you are done solving each problem, check your math and make sure you answered the question.

1. Jill and Bob were playing a game. When Jill said a number, Bob did something to the number to get a different number. Look at the numbers they said.

   What number did Jill say if Bob said the number 4?

   Explain how you arrived at your answer.

Jill	Bob
30	6
25	5
15	3
40	8

2. On March 16th, three boys went to the store. They each brought $5 to spend. They left for the store at 9 o'clock. They returned home at 12 o'clock. How much money did they have to spend in all?

Whole-Class Practice 10

Show your work. Let the person who is grading your paper know what you were thinking as you solved the problems. Read each problem carefully. When you are done solving each problem, check your math and make sure you answered the question.

1. Patti has seven coins which total $0.38. What are the coins?

2. A barnyard has 34 legs belonging to 11 animals. Some are cows and the rest are chickens. Determine exactly how many cows and how many chickens are in the barnyard.

Independent Practice Cards

Students can work on the task cards individually, with partners, or in groups. Remind them of the steps for successful problem solving before they begin.

The purpose of the task cards is to provide students with immediate feedback. They are to solve the problems on the cards and bring them to the teacher to check if they have solved the problems correctly. A parent volunteer or capable student can also serve as checker so the teacher is free to move about the room offering assistance where needed.

To prepare practice cards, copy each Independent Practice Card page. Cut along the dashed lines. Fold along the solid line to create a card with problem 1 on one side and problem 2 on the other. Staple, glue, or tape the card at the top.

Students should not get credit for a correct answer if they did not show their work. Tell them you will check their answers after they have shown their work.

Independent Practice Card 1

Show your work. Read each problem carefully. When you are done solving each problem, check your math and make sure you answered the question.

1. Roy bought nine tapes for $3 each and eight packages of batteries for $2 each. (Prices include tax.) If he pays for items with a $50 bill, how much change would he receive?

---

2. Jennifer wants to build a rectangular fence around her garden that is six feet by 10 feet. How many feet of fencing does she need to go all around her garden?

Independent Practice Card 1 (cont.)

Independent Practice Card 2

Show your work. Read each problem carefully. When you are done solving each problem, check your math and make sure you answered the question.

1. Starting with the number 23, Cindy counts forward eight odd numbers. At what number does she stop?

Independent Practice Card 2 (cont.)

2. David's family paid $175 a week to rent a car. They rented the car for three weeks. How much did it cost to rent the car for the three weeks?

Independent Practice Card 3

Show your work. Read each problem carefully. When you are done solving each problem, check your math and make sure you answered the question.

1. It took Ethan 50 minutes to put together a jigsaw puzzle. He started at 5:35 P.M. and worked without stopping. What time was it when he was done putting together the puzzle?

Independent Practice Card 3 (cont.)

2. The graph shows how many magazines the fourth graders sold during a fundraiser for their school. If they earned $3 for each magazine they sold, how much money did they earn in March?

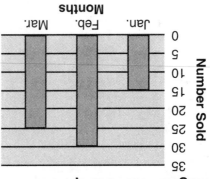

Magazine Subscriptions Sold

Independent Practice Card 4

Show your work. Read each problem carefully. When you are done solving each problem, check your math and make sure you answered the question.

1. Stan bought six books that cost $2 each and four books that cost $3 each. (Prices include tax.) If he pays for the books with two twenty dollar bills, how much change would he receive?

Independent Practice Card 4 (cont.)

2. Janet wants to sew trim on a square scarf that is 12 inches on each side. How many inches of trim does she need to buy?

If the trim costs 5¢ an inch, how much does she have to spend to buy the trim for her scarf?

Independent Practice Card 5

Show your work. Read each problem carefully. When you are done solving each problem, check your math and make sure you answered the question.

1. Tony works at a fast-food restaurant. He sold 33 hamburgers one hour, 78 hamburgers the next hour, and 32 hamburgers the last hour. Using front-end estimation, estimate the total number of hamburgers he sold.

Independent Practice Card 5 (cont.)

2. Look at these dominoes.

  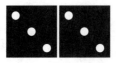

Which of the dominoes below could be included in this group?

A.    B.    C.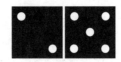

Explain why you think as you do.

Independent Practice Card 6

Show your work. Read each problem carefully. When you are done solving each problem, check your math and make sure you answered the question.

1. Make the greatest sum possible with these digits: 4, 7, 8, and 5. Put each of these digits in one of the boxes below to make 2 two-digit numbers.

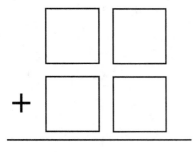

---

2. Starting at the number 30, Joy counts forward five even numbers. At what number does she stop?

Independent Practice Card 6 (cont.)

Independent Practice Card 7

Show your work. Read each problem carefully. When you are done solving each problem, check your math and make sure you answered the question.

1. Look at the table of number pairs. Which rule could you use on each number in Column A to get the number in Column B?

A	B
3	10
5	16
7	22
9	28

Independent Practice Card 7 (cont.)

2. Your teacher says you can take a piece of candy from one of two different bags, a blue bag and a red bag, but you have to choose without looking. Your favorite kind of candy is butterscotch. In the blue bag eight out of 10 pieces are butterscotch. In the red bag 10 out of 20 pieces are butterscotch. From which bag do you have a better chance of getting butterscotch? Explain your answer.

Independent Practice Card 8

Show your work. Read each problem carefully. When you are done solving each problem, check your math and make sure you answered the question.

1. Andy works at a pizza place. His hourly wage is $5.00 an hour. He works 20 hours each week. How much money is he paid each week?

Independent Practice Card 8 (cont.)

2. A group of 35 Cub Scouts is planning a trip to the Air Force museum. Parents will be driving them in their cars. Each parent can drive four Cub Scouts. How many parents are needed to drive all Cub Scouts?

Independent Practice Card 9

Show your work. Read each problem carefully. When you are done solving each problem, check your math and make sure you answered the question.

1. What prime number, when first multiplied by 7, then added to 7, then divided by 2, equals 21?

---

2. Mrs. Jacobson has 30 students in her class. She has four more boys than girls. How many boys and girls are in Mrs. Jacobson's class?

Independent Practice Card 9 (cont.)

Independent Practice Card 10

Show your work. Read each problem carefully. When you are done solving each problem, check your math and make sure you answered the question.

1. Marco earns $8.00 an hour bagging groceries at the supermarket. He worked 18.5 hours last week. How much money did he make last week?

2. Ellen bought a sweater for $35.00. If the sweater was on sale for 30% off, what was the original price of the sweater that Ellen bought?

Independent Practice Card 10 (cont.)

Practice Sheets

Practice sheets are different from the Independent Practice cards in that students work all the problems on a sheet at one time and do not get immediate feedback.

The teacher should move about the room to observe the students as they work. Remind students to use the problem-solving steps and to show all work in the space provided. The teacher should watch to see that all students are engaged in the problem-solving process. Students should understand that learning how to solve the problems is as important than getting the right answers.

Encourage students to work together to solve the problems on the practice sheets.

Practice Sheet 1

Show your work. Read each problem carefully. When you are done solving each problem, check your math and make sure you answered the question.

1. In the first week it is open, a video store sells 52 video games. In its second week it sells 15 more video games than it sold the first week. How many video games did the video store sell in the two weeks?

2. Frankie is saving money to buy a birthday gift for his mother. So far he has saved $14.45. If he wants to buy his mother a picture frame that costs $21.20 (price already includes tax), how much more does he need to save?

3. The average life span of a grizzly bear is 25 years. The Asian elephant has an average life span 15 years longer than a grizzly bear. The average life span of a box turtle is 60 years longer than the Asian elephant. What is the average life span of the Asian elephant and the box turtle?

Practice Sheet 1 *(cont.)*

4. If five packages of pencils cost $2.50, how much do six packages of pencils cost? (Price includes tax.)

5. Tom had 30 cookies. He divided the cookies equally into five boxes. Then he gave one of the boxes to a friend. How many cookies did Tom have left?

6. Jon and Peter had seven cookies each. Catherine had four cookies, and Alex had six cookies. They put all of the cookies in one big pile. Then they divided them into equal piles and each one took a pile. How many cookies did each of them get?

Practice Sheet 2

Show your work. Read each problem carefully. When you are done solving each problem, check your math and make sure you answered the question.

1. John took a straw that was 12 inches long and bent it into a square shape. What is the length of each side?

2. Jason made three dozen cupcakes. He kept six for his family and sold the rest for 25¢ each. How much money did Jason make selling the cupcakes?

3. Kelly wants to buy muffins for her class. The muffins are sold eight muffins to a box. There are 28 students in her class. How many boxes of muffins should she buy to have enough muffins for everyone in her class?

Practice Sheet 2 *(cont.)*

4. A store sells books for $3.00 each. If you buy two, you get 25¢ off the price of each book. How much would it cost to buy two books at that store?

5. Four friends have 12 trading cards each. Their names are Eric, Jeff, Zach, and Josh. Eric gives three of his cards to Jeff. Zach gives 2 of his cards to Josh. How many cards does each person have after they traded?

6. The perimeter of a rectangle is 32 inches. The length of the rectangle is 10 inches. What is the width of the rectangle?

Practice Sheet 3

Show your work. Read each problem carefully. When you are done solving each problem, check your math and make sure you answered the question.

1. A square cage is made of 20 feet of wire fencing. How long is each side of the cage?

2. A school ordered 60 workbooks. The workbooks are packed 20 to a box. How many boxes arrived at the school?

    If they ordered 55 workbooks instead, then how many boxes would arrive at the school?

3. The perimeter of a rectangle is 24 inches. The length of the rectangle is eight inches. What is the width of the rectangle?

Practice Sheet 3 *(cont.)*

4. A store sells comic books for $2.00 each. If you buy two, you get 50¢ off the total price. If you buy three, you get 75¢ off the total price. If you buy four, you get $1 off the total price. How much would it cost to buy 4 comic books?

5. The Bulldogs soccer team scored a total of 11 points. Three players scored 2 points each. How many points did the other players score?

6. Olivia bought Valentine's Day cards for her class. The cards are sold 12 to a box. Not counting her, there are 21 students in her class. How many boxes of Valentine's Day cards should she buy to have enough cards for everyone in her class?

Practice Sheet 4

Show your work. Read each problem carefully. When you are done solving each problem, check your math and make sure you answered the question.

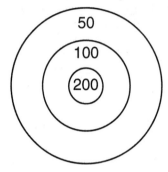

1. If you had four darts to throw at the dartboard above, what is the highest possible score you could get?

2. If you had four darts to throw at the dartboard above, and you hit the dartboard each time, what is the lowest score you could get?

3. You had four darts to throw at the dartboard above, and you hit the dartboard each time. Your total score is 250. What section did you hit three times?

Practice Sheet 4 (cont.)

4. A movie was shown two times, starting at 7:30 P.M. The movie lasted one hour and a half. There was a half-hour between each showing. At what time does the second showing start?

5. Mrs. Brown ordered four 25-lb. bags of black oil sunflower birdseed and two 10-lb. bags of thistle birdseed. What was the total weight of Mrs. Brown's birdseed order?

6. For Halloween, Sam wanted to make a border of orange ribbon to go around his front window. The window was 3 ft. wide and 5 ft. high. How much ribbon did he need?

Practice Sheet 5

Show your work. Read each problem carefully. When you are done solving each problem, check your math and make sure you answered the question.

1. Four boys went fishing on October 15th. They walked two miles to get to the fishing spot. They each caught three fish. How many fish did the four boys catch in all?

2. Maggie and Tommy took a trip with their family to visit their grandma. They had to drive for two days to get there. They traveled 245 miles the first day. They traveled 323 miles the second day. They stayed at their grandma's a week, then drove back. How many miles did they travel to get there and back?

3. Jake buys a candy bar that costs $0.59. (Price includes tax.) He paid for the candy bar using no more than 10 coins. One possible combination of coins he could have used would be two quarters, one nickel, and four pennies. What are two other combinations of coins he could have used?

Practice Sheet 5 *(cont.)*

Money Earned by Mrs. Kerr's Class

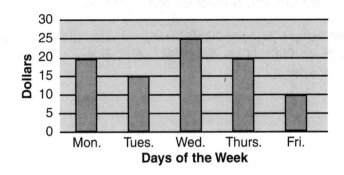

4. The graph shows the amount of money Mrs. Kerr's class earned for their school each day of their fundraiser. How much money did they earn in all five days?

5. Rose has $10 to spend at the store. She buys two pens that cost $1.79 each, a magazine that costs $2.55, and two erasers that cost $0.29 each. (Prices include tax.) What change should she receive if she pays with a $10 bill?

6. Ben took a straw that was 40 centimeters long. He bent it into a square. How long was each side?

Practice Sheet 6

Show your work. Read each problem carefully. When you are done solving each problem, check your math and make sure you answered the question.

1. On December 19th, five boys went to the store. They each brought $8 to spend. They left for the store at 4 o'clock. They returned home at 6 o'clock. How much money did the five boys have to spend in all?

2. Katie and Jen live in Columbus, Ohio. They took a trip to visit their grandma. The trip took three days. They traveled 326 miles the first day. They traveled 258 miles on the second day. Finally, on the third day they reached their grandma's house after traveling 178 miles that day. How many miles did they travel in all?

3. Tory buys a candy bar that costs $0.77. (Price includes tax.) Show three ways she can pay for the candy bar using no more than 10 coins.

Practice Sheet 6 *(cont.)*

4. The average cost of gasoline this month is $1.39. The average cost of gasoline last month was $1.27. What is the difference between the average cost of gasoline of these two months?

5. Your teacher asked you to toss a pair of dice 100 times. You are told to add the numbers at the top of the dice and record your answers. Explain why you would be more likely to get a 6, 7, or 8 than a 2 or a 12.

Practice Sheet 7

Show your work. Read each problem carefully. When you are done solving each problem, check your math and make sure you answered the question.

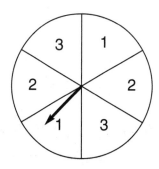

1. You and a friend are using this spinner to play a game. Your friend says he will spin the arrow 20 times. If the arrow lands on an odd number, he gets a point. If the arrow lands on an even number, you get a point. The winner is the person with the most points. Is this a fair game? Explain whether one of you has a better chance of winning.

2. Sandy invited five friends over for a sleepover. She had a bag of cookies to share with her friends and herself. There were 18 cookies in the bag. How many cookies did each girl get?

Practice Sheet 7 *(cont.)*

3. Andrew bought four packs of paper that cost $1.79 each. He paid for them with a $10 bill. (Price includes tax.) What was his change?

4. Sales tax on an item that costs $1.00 would be $0.05. Sales tax on an item that costs $2.00 would be $0.10. Sales tax on an item that costs $3.00 would be $0.15. If the pattern continues, what would the sales tax be on an item that cost $5.00?

5. Phil is told his school building is 20 times his height. If Phil's height is 4 feet, how high is his school building?

Practice Sheet 8

Show your work. Read each problem carefully. When you are done solving each problem, check your math and make sure you answered the question.

1. You are playing a game with marbles in two bags. The brown bag contains the following marbles:

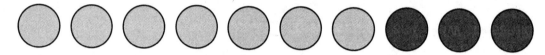

The white bag contains the following marbles:

You get to stay in the game if you pick out a gray marble without looking. From which bag are you more likely to draw out a gray marble? Explain your answer.

2. Monica received $20 for her birthday. She used her money to buy items that cost $2.00, $3.25, $8.25, and $1.00. Use front-end estimation to figure out about how much money she had left.

Practice Sheet 8 (cont.)

3. Make the greatest sum possible with these digits: 7, 8, 2, and 4. Put each of these digits in one of the boxes below to make 2 two-digit numbers.

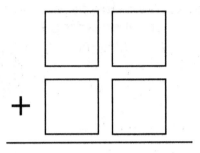

4. Rebecca looks at the clock and sees that it is 3:00 P.M. She needs to be home by 4:30. How much time does she have before she needs to be home?

5. Jessy wants to build a fence around her rectangular shaped garden that is 5 feet by 6 feet. How many feet of fencing does she need to go all around her garden?

If the fencing costs $2.00 a foot, how much does she have to spend to buy the fencing?

Practice Sheet 9

Show your work. Read each problem carefully. When you are done solving each problem, check your math and make sure you answered the question.

1. Andrea got a $50 bill from her grandparents for her birthday. She bought a portable CD player for $36 and two packages of batteries for $3 each. (Prices include tax.) If she pays for all the items with the $50 bill, how much change would she receive?

2. It took Brandy and Maura 35 minutes to put together a jigsaw puzzle. If they started it at 1:50 P.M. and worked without stopping, what time was it when they were done putting together the puzzle?

3. Rachel has a square piece of graph paper that is 10 cm by 10 cm. She starts with a corner square and colors every other square around the edge. How many squares does she color?

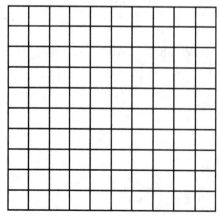

Practice Sheet 9 (cont.)

4. Charlene worked 105 hours babysitting last summer. If she earned $3.00 per hour, how much money did she earn?

5. The fine for a late book at the library is 10¢ the first day and 2¢ for each additional day. What is the fine for a book that is 2 weeks late?

6. Nikki wants to buy 20 pencils. Which store has the lowest price for pencils? Explain why you think as you do.

Store A	Store B	Store C
1 for 10¢	2 for 18¢	5 for 40¢

Practice Sheet 10

Directions: Solve the following logical reasoning word problems. If needed, use diagrams to process the information that each problem provides. Show your work on the back of this paper.

1. Sherry, Tommy, and Mara are classmates. Sherry's birthday is one week after Tommy's. Mara's birthday is two days before Tommy's. If Tommy's birthday is September 10th, when are Mara and Sherry's birthdays?

   _____

   _____

2. In Mr. Johnson's first-grade class, Natalie wants to sit by Noriko but not by Leo in the first row of desks. If Charlie sits in the first desk and Mary sits in the second desk, in what order will the three other students sit?

   _____

   _____

3. The Connor family went to get hamburgers at the Hamburger Shack. Jessica ordered a hamburger with tomatoes and pickles. Her sister Lauren ordered a hamburger with mustard and lettuce. Mr. Connor ordered a hamburger with pickles and onions. Mrs. Connor ordered a hamburger with tomatoes and pickles. Which family members ordered the same type of hamburger?

   _____

   _____

4. The town of Millerville is adding a new street to their town. On the new street, they will be adding a new town hall, library, bank, and post office. If the post office cannot be built next to the library, and the town hall must be the first building, and the post office must be the last building on the street, what is the order of the buildings on the new street?

   _____

   _____

Practice Sheet 10 *(cont.)*

5. Lynette is taller than Mark but not as tall as Sally. Robin is taller than Sally. Who is the tallest? _____

6. Nicholas is stronger than Robin but not as strong as Lynette. Daryl is not as strong as Robin. Who is the strongest? _____ Who is the weakest? _____

7. Sally ate more than Lynette but not as much as Nicholas. Daryl ate less than Lynette. Who ate the most? _____ Who ate the least? _____

8. Tyler jumped farther than Daryl but not as far as Lynette. Maria jumped farther than Lynette but not as far as Nicholas. Who jumped the farthest? _____ Who jumped the shortest distance? _____

9. Daryl slept longer than Tyler but not as long as Sally. Lynette slept longer than Sally but not as long as Robin. Who slept the longest?_____ Who had the least sleep? _____

10. Lance is shorter than Lynette but not as short as Sally. Daryl is shorter than Sally but not as short as Nicholas. Robin is not as short as Lynette. Who is the shortest?

    _____

11. Maya likes to read short stories and poetry. Lisa likes to read poetry, nonfiction, and science fiction books. Laurel likes to read short stories and mystery novels. Who likes to read poetry? _____

12. Daryl reads faster than Mark but not as fast as Tyler. Maria reads faster than Tyler but not as fast as Lynette. Lance reads faster than Lynette but not as fast as Robin. Nicholas reads faster than Robin. Write the order from slowest to fastest reader.

    _____

Homework Sets

The homework sheets provide students with the opportunity to practice their problem-solving skills without the support of the teacher and classmates. Some students will need more support at home than others. Prior to sending the homework sheets home, you can send home the letter to the parents explaining the purpose of these assignments and suggestions on ways they can help.

Parent Letter

Dear Parents,

Mathematics today is not just arithmetic and basic skills. Students are required to demonstrate their ability to understand and explain math concepts. They need to be able to solve a variety of math problems and apply problem-solving strategies. Today's math instruction is designed to help students communicate their ideas and to make connections to real-life situations.

We have been working in math class to develop these skills. Your child will be bringing home worksheets that will help them practice these skills. They have been taught to show their work. This is especially important because partial credit will be given when they get an answer wrong but have shown correct thinking in their work.

Some children experience frustration when solving problems. They need to know that it is okay to feel this way. It is important for them to develop the ability to persist when a problem is difficult, to see past the confusion and struggle a bit rather than just give up.

You can help your child by . . .

- providing a good place to do homework away from distractions, such as the TV.

- being positive about your child's efforts.

- offering guidance, not answers, if your child is experiencing difficulty.

- asking your child to read the question out loud.

- helping your child think about what information is already known.

- asking your child to write his or her ideas on paper and to share out loud what he or she is thinking.

- asking your child to reread the question and to check that the question has been answered.

Please don't hesitate to call if you have any questions or concerns. Your encouragement and guidance is invaluable.

Sincerely,

_____

Homework Set 1

Remember to show your work. You need to be able to show what you are thinking as you solve each problem. When you are done solving a problem, check your math and make sure you answered the question. Write your answers on the lines provided.

1. If you put 25 cents in a piggy bank every day for the month of September, how much money would you have at the end of the month?

_____

2. It takes Ellen's father 35 minutes to drive to work. He leaves for work at 6:45 A.M. and drives straight to work. What time is it when he arrives at work?

_____

3. John bought two books at $1.95 each, and two books at $2.95 each. (Prices include tax.) He paid for the books with a twenty-dollar bill. How much change did he receive?

_____

Homework Set 1 *(cont.)*

4. Samantha wants to buy cupcakes for her class. The cupcakes are sold six cupcakes to a box. There are 22 students in her class. How many boxes of cupcakes should she buy to have enough cupcakes for everyone in her class?

_____

5. Tony is building a frame for a square cage that is 4 feet by 4 feet. He wants to put wire around it. How much wire does he need to buy to have enough to go around all the sides?

_____

6. Terry is buying Valentine's Day cards for her class. The cards are sold 20 to a box. Not counting her, there are 27 students in her class. How many boxes of Valentine's Day cards should she buy to have enough cards for everyone in her class?

_____

Homework Set 2

Remember to show your work. You need to be able to show what you are thinking as you solve each problem. When you are done solving a problem, check your math and make sure you answered the question. Write your answers on the lines provided.

1. Mr. and Mrs. Smith and their children, ages 6, 10, and 12, are going to the movie theater. They need to buy five tickets. Figure out the total amount they will spend on the tickets if the tickets for the movie cost:

Adults	$6.00
Children ages 6 and up	$4.00
Children under 6	Free

_____

2. Ben goes to the school book fair with $10 to spend. He wants to buy books that cost $1.39, $2.79, and $2.19. Show how Ben could use rounding to the nearest dollar to estimate how much the books would cost. Does he have enough money to buy all three books?

_____

3. Janet is having a pizza party at her house. She wants to buy enough pizza for herself and her seven friends. The pizzas are cut into eight equal pieces. She figures each girl will eat two pieces of pizza. How many pizzas should she buy?

_____

4. The graph shows the amount of money Mrs. Smith's class earned each day of their fund-raiser. How much money did they earn in all five days?

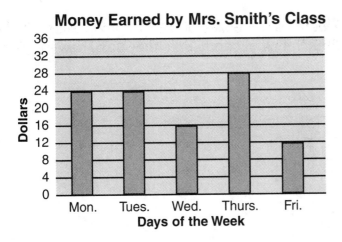

Money Earned by Mrs. Smith's Class

_____

5. Every spring, the students at Colonial Hills Elementary compete during field day, a day of races and other track events. Students are awarded prizes for coming in first, second, or third place. This year the second grade won five prizes, the third grade won two times as many prizes as the second grade, and the fourth grade won 3 times as many prizes as the third grade. How many prizes did the fourth grade win?

_____

Homework Set 3

Remember to show your work. You need to be able to show what you are thinking as you solve each problem. When you are done solving a problem, check your math and make sure you answered the question. Write your answers on the lines provided.

1. The students at Stevenson Elementary were selling boxes of candy bars to raise money for their library. If they earned $2.00 for each box of candy bars they sold, how much money did they raise?

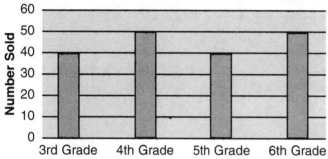

Number of Candy Bar Boxes Sold

_____

2. Jenny is writing all the numbers from 1 to 100. How many times will she write the number 2?

_____

3. Tory buys two paintbrushes at $1.90 each. She buys five jars of paint for $0.99 each. She gave the clerk a $20 bill. How much change should she receive?

_____

Homework Set 3 (cont.)

4. Jason and Aaron are eating small pizzas. Their pizzas are exactly the same size. Jason cut his pizza into six pieces and ate four of the pieces. Aaron cut his pizza into eight pieces and ate four of them. Who ate more pizza? Explain your answer.

_____

_____

_____

_____

_____

                                                                    _____

5. Shannon has $10.00. She goes shopping at a store and sees these items on sale. What are the three different items she could spend her money on if she wants to spend all of her money? Does she get any change back? If so, how much? (All item prices already include tax.)

| hair accessories $1.75 | journals $4.99 | stuffed animals $6.99 | magnets $2.49 |

_____

_____

_____

_____

                                                                    _____

Homework Set 4 (cont.)

Remember to show your work. You need to be able to show what you are thinking as you solve each problem. When you are done solving a problem, check your math and make sure you answered the question. Write your answers on the lines provided.

1. The diameter of a quarter is about one inch. How many quarters could fit across a table that was four feet wide?

_____

2. The pay phone at the drugstore is used about 60 times a day. At that rate, how many times is it used in a week?

_____

3. Jessie put a dime in an empty piggy bank on Sunday, two dimes on Monday, three dimes on Tuesday, four dimes on Wednesday, five dimes on Thursday, six dimes on Friday, and seven dimes on Saturday. How much money did she have in her piggy bank at the end of the week?

_____

Homework Set 4 *(cont.)*

4. What's the number? It's less than 49 but greater than 31. It is an even number. It is also a multiple of 5.

_____

5. Barbie bought three bags of candy that cost $1.89 each. (Price includes tax.) She paid for them with a $10 bill. What was her change?

_____

6. Which is a better deal, five packs of gum at 35¢ each or a package that contains five packs of gum for $1.90? Explain your answer.

_____

_____

_____

_____

Homework Set 5

Remember to show your work. You need to be able to show what you are thinking as you solve each problem. When you are done solving a problem, check your math and make sure you answered the question. Write your answers on the lines provided.

1. The Miller family went bowling on January 11th. They left their house at 2:15 P.M. and returned home at 4:30 P.M. There are five people in the family. It cost $2.50 per person to bowl one game. How much did it cost if all five family members bowled one game?

   _____

2. The PTA is having a cake sale. On the first day they sold 20 cakes, on the second day they sold 14 more cakes than they sold on the first day. How many total cakes did the PTA sell on both days?

   _____

3. Ross is going to visit his grandparents. If he drives at 60 mph for 86 miles, how long will it take him to get to his grandparents house?

   _____

Homework Set 5 *(cont.)*

4. The diameter of Venus is 7,521 miles wide. The diameter of Earth is 405 miles longer than the diameter of Venus. The diameter of Mercury is 4,894 miles shorter than the diameter of Earth. What is the diameter of Mercury and Earth?

_____

5. Shelly is buying things at the grocery store that she will need for her birthday party. She has $40 to spend. She buys two 12-packs of soda for $3.50 each. She buys three bags of chips for $2.79 each. She buys a cake for $14.99. (Prices include tax.) How much does she spend in all?

_____

6. Raymond baked 38 cookies. He equally divided as many cookies as possible into 4. He gave away the cookies that were left over. How many cookies did Raymond give away?

_____

Homework Set 6

Remember to show your work. You need to be able to show what you are thinking as you solve each problem. When you are done solving a problem, check your math and make sure you answered the question. Write your answers on the lines provided.

1. David and Jenny each had 15 pieces of candy. Nick had 12 pieces of candy, and Casey had six pieces of candy. They put all of the pieces of candy in one big pile. Then they divided them into equal piles and each one took a pile. How many pieces of candy did each of them get?

_____

2. The students at Sharon Elementary were raising money for their school. They collected used books to sell at a sale for 25¢ each. The graph below shows how many books were collected on each day. If they sold all the books they collected, how much money did they raise for the school?

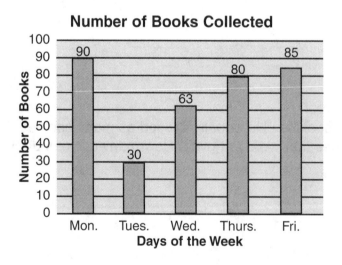

Number of Books Collected

_____

Homework Set 6 (cont.)

3. Keara took a pipe cleaner that was 28 cm long. She bent it into a square shape. How long was each side of her square?

_____

4. You reach into a bag of marbles that contains 14 white marbles and 6 blue marbles. You pull out a blue marble. Predict the color of marble you are likely to get the second time you reach in the bag. Explain your answer.

_____

_____

_____

5. A group of 28 students, one teacher, and six parents took a field trip to the art museum. The teacher and each of the six parents drove the children in their cars. Each car had an equal amount of students. How many students went in each car?

_____

Homework Set 7

Remember to show your work. You need to be able to show what you are thinking as you solve each problem. When you are done solving a problem, check your math and make sure you answered the question. Write your answers on the lines provided.

1. Katie babysits for her brothers every day after school. Her wage is $5.00 an hour. You want to find out how much money Katie is paid each week. What piece of information do you need to help you find out?

   _____

   _____

   _____

   _____

2. Read the sentences. Circle each sentence that tells how all the figures below are alike.

   - They are polygons.

   - They have curved sides.

   - They have at least one line of symmetry.

   - They have at least one right angle.

3. Sixteen pennies laid end to end equal a foot. You can put 32 pennies across the width of your desk. How many feet wide is your desk?

_____

4. Make the smallest sum possible with these digits: 4, 7, 8, 1. Put each of these digits in one of the boxes below to make 2 two-digit numbers.

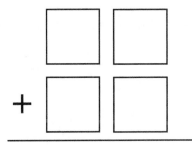

_____

5. Ellen and Anne were playing a game. When Ellen said a number, Anne did something to the number to get a different number. Look at the numbers they said.

Ellen	Anne
5	25
7	35
9	45
3	15

What number did Anne say if Ellen said the number 6?   _____

Explain how you arrived at your answer.

_____

_____

_____

_____

Homework Set 8

Remember to show your work. You need to be able to show what you are thinking as you solve each problem. When you are done solving a problem, check your math and make sure you answered the question. Write your answers on the lines provided.

1. Mrs. Patterson needed to buy 80 doughnuts for a class party. The doughnuts are packed 12 to a box. How many boxes does she need to buy?

   _____

   If the doughnuts cost $3.99 a box, how much will she spend?

   _____

2. Ned bought two shirts for $12.25 each, and a pair of pants for $14.99. (Prices include tax.) How much change will he receive if he pays the cashier with a $50 bill?

   _____

3. At the bake sale, cookies are 10¢ each and cupcakes are 25¢ each. Denise bought four cookies and two cupcakes. How much money did she spend?

   _____

Homework Set 8 *(cont.)*

4. Mr. Gilbert has 25 students in his class. He asked the students to choose their favorite pet given the choice of cats, dogs, hamsters, or fish. Then he made a graph of the information. How many students did not choose a favorite pet?

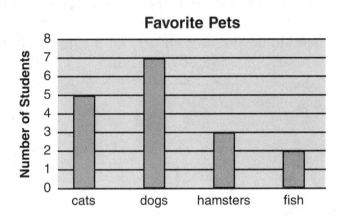

Favorite Pets

_____

5. Shelly wants to buy three notebooks for school. Which store has the lowest price for notebooks? Explain your answer.

Store A	Store B	Store C
3 for $3.99	1 for $1.49	1 for $1.29

_____

_____

_____

_____

_____

_____

Homework Set 9

Remember to show your work. You need to be able to show what you are thinking as you solve each problem. When you are done solving a problem, check your math and make sure you answered the question. Write your answers on the lines provided.

1. Christian wants to give a package of fruit snack to each person on his soccer team. The fruit snacks are sold in packages of six. There are 14 people on his team. How many packages would he need to buy to have enough for each person on his team and have one for himself?

   _____

2. Edison Elementary School is having a pizza party for its second, third, and fourth graders. The second grade ate 8 pizzas. The third grade ate 4 more pizzas than the second grade. The fourth grade ate twice as many pizzas as the third grade class. How many pizzas did the fourth graders eat?

   _____

3. A cafeteria sells small pizzas for $0.99. A small drink costs $0.89. (Prices include tax.) Three friends each order a small pizza and small drink for lunch. How much did they spend altogether?

   _____

4. Three fifth grade classes sold gift wrap to raise money for a school project. The regular gift wrap cost $3.00 each and the foil wrap cost $6.00 each. The total amount of rolls sold by each class is shown by the graph below. What information is missing for you to figure out how much money each class raised?

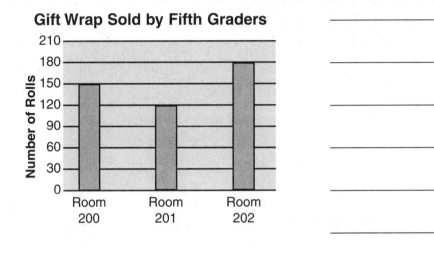

5. Raymond is using a shoebox to display a scene of a book he has read for class. The top of the shoebox is 4 inches by 10 inches. He wants to use a piece of cardboard to make a flat roof for his box. He wants the roof to stick out 1 inch over the edge of the box on all four sides. How big would the piece of cardboard be?

Homework Set 10

Directions: Solve each problem.

1. LaTonya worked 6 hours each on Monday, Wednesday, and Friday; she worked 10 hours each on Tuesday and Thursday. How many hours did she work altogether? _____
If she earns $7 an hour, how much money did she earn? _____

2. Which expression shows the total cost of 4 items at $7 each and 5 items at $6 each?
_____ What is the total cost? _____

   a. (4 + 5) x (6 + 7)   c. (7 x 5) – (6 x 4)
   b. (4 x $7) + (5 x $6)   d. (4 + 7) ÷ (5 + 6)

3. Which expression shows the total weight of two crates that weigh 25 pounds each, four crates that weigh 40 pounds each, and five crates that each weigh 30 pounds. _____
What is the total weight? _____

   a. 25 + 40 + 30   c. (25 x 4) + (40 x 30)
   b. (2 + 4 + 5) x (25 + 40 + 30)   d. (2 x 25) + (4 x 40) + (5 x 30)

4. A clock is set correctly at 1:00 P.M. It loses 3 minutes every hour. What will the clock read when the correct time is 10:00 P.M.? _____

5. Four boys work together painting houses for the summer. For each house they paint, they are paid $256.00. If the boys work for four months and their expenses are $152.00 per month, how many houses must they paint for each of them to have one thousand dollars at the end of the summer? _____

Homework Set 10 *(cont.)*

6. The peel of a banana weighs about 1/8 of the total weight of the banana. This is a little heavier than the peel of most fruit. If you buy 3 kg of bananas in a wood basket at $0.60 per kg, about how much are you paying for the banana peel? _____ How much for the banana itself? (Round to the nearest cent.) _____

7. James bought a video game for $29.95. He bought a computer CD-ROM game for $19.95. Both games were on sale for 25% off the ticketed price. How much did James spend on the video game and CD-ROM? _____ How much did he save? _____

8. Laurel and Joey went shopping for a birthday gift for their parents. They decided to buy a picture frame that costs $22.50. Laurel paid for 60% of the gift, and Joey paid for 40% of the gift. How much did each person pay for the gift? _____

9. Erin needs to buy 2 sheets of plywood, 6 dowels, and 3 two-by-fours for a building project. The plywood costs $2.65 per sheet, the dowels $0.39 each, and the two-by-fours $0.89 each. How much is her subtotal, without tax? _____

10. Bob bought a new bike. The bike cost $129.95 with tax. He gave the cashier $150.00. The bike also comes with a $10.00 mail-in rebate. How much will Bob get back, including the rebate? _____

11. Yvonne travels 4.8 miles to get to town. Once there, she drives 3.7 miles to run her errands. After she returns home, she realizes she forgot to go to the pet store for some special fish food. This trip to the pet store is 6.2 miles. Once she finally reaches home after all her errands, the odometer on the car reads 36,835.3 miles. What did the odometer read before she started for town the first time? _____

12. Mrs. Carlson wants to be sure all of the students have equal access to the Halloween candy she brought to share throughout the day. She has two packages each of Peanut Butter Buddies, Chocolate Chewies, and Caramel Creamies. The Peanut Butter Buddies have an estimated 24 pieces per bag, the Chocolate Chewies about 36 per bag, and the Caramel Creamies about 30 pieces per bag. Mrs. Carlson plans to place one bowl of mixed candy at each of six sets of tables in her classroom. About how many pieces of candy will each bowl have? _____

13. In an elementary school, the kindergarten through third grade classes, of which there are four students in each grade level, receive 30 minutes daily of instruction time for special classes such as art, music, drama, gym, etc. The fourth and fifth grade classes, of which there are five in each grade level, receive 40 minutes daily for special classes. How many total hours of the school day do all the classes spend in special classes?

_____

14. Kiki's class sold school pens for a fund-raiser. They sold 12 boxes for a total of 1,728 pens. How many pens are in each box?

15. At the end of the day, Mrs. Marcus gives some students a reward of two pieces of red-hot candy balls. On Monday, she gave out a total of 18 candies. How many students received the reward on Monday?

Problem-Solving Tests

Although students have been encouraged to work together during most of the problem-solving activities, it is important that you measure each student's success at problem-solving. Use this test to measure your students' mastery of problem-solving techniques.

Remind students to do their own work on the test and to try their best so that you can get an accurate picture of their proficiency at problem solving.

Tips and Strategies for Math Tests

Open-ended Math Tests

The first three math tests will measure how well you can apply the problem-solving strategies that you have been practicing in class. It is important that you do your best so that you give an accurate picture of how well you can solve problems. It is also important that you do your own work on this test.

Remember

- Read each problem carefully.
- Show your work to let the grader know what you were thinking as you solved the problems.

- Be persistent. (Don't give up!)
- Put your ideas down on paper to help you solve each problem.
- Check your work.

Multiple-Choice Math Tests

The last three math tests will help you apply your skills and strategies on the types of questions that you might see on standardized math tests.

Introduction

To perform your best on the mathematics section of a standardized test, you need not know the right answer every time. But you do need to use two important strategies that will improve your score: estimating and recognizing a reasonable answer.

Here's the Idea

Estimating is a way of getting close to a right answer by rounding. When you round numbers in a problem, you will get an answer that is close to the right answer.

Recognizing a reasonable answer means deciding that an answer choice is probably right, based on what you already know about numbers and problems. You can drop some answer choices right away because they are not reasonable.

However, before we look at these two skills, below are some tips that apply to taking any test, whether it is in language arts, math, science, or social studies. These tips will be repeated because they are important!

Test-Taking Tips

- Read directions carefully before marking any test questions, even though you have done that kind of test before. You may think you already know what the directions say, but don't ignore them—read them over. If you don't understand the directions, raise your hand and ask for help. Although your teacher must read the directions exactly as they are written, the teacher can make sure you understand what the directions mean.

- Follow instructions. Pay close attention to the sample exercises. They will help you understand what the items on the test will be like and how to mark your answer sheet properly.

- Read the entire question and all the answer choices. Do not stop reading when you have found a correct answer. Choices "D" or "E" may read "B and C" or "all of the above." On some tests, two answers are both correct. You need to read all the answer choices before marking your answer.

- And remember—taking a test is not a race! There are no prizes for finishing first. Use all of the time provided for the test. If you have time left over, check your answers.

Tips and Strategies for Math Tests

Multiple-Choice Math Tests *(cont.)*

Note: There is a range of different concepts and skills varying from one test to the next. The tests do not range from easy to difficult from test to test or within each test. They are varied in the types of word problems and skills being assessed.

Try and Discuss

Now let's discuss those two skills for mathematics tests—*estimating* and *recognizing a reasonable answer*. When you estimate, you use round numbers to come close to the correct answer without even working the problem through. Use these two rules for rounding:

- Round <u>up</u> for numbers greater than five.
- Round <u>down</u> for numbers less than five.

For example, round the numbers in this problem to find the answer—do not work the problem on paper! Just round the numbers in your mind.

23 + 16 =

(A) 7
(B) 29
(C) 39
(D) 216

Fill in the correct circle.

Ⓐ   Ⓑ   Ⓒ   Ⓓ

Remember the rules of rounding. Round down 23 to 20 because 3 is less than 5. Then round up 16 to 20 because 6 is greater than 5. That makes the problem in your mind 20 + 20 = (?). The answer to that problem is 40. Which answer choice is closest to 40?

You can use estimating for very large problems, too. Try this one:

2,379
+ 4,675

(A) 7,054
(B) 8,987
(C) 3,465
(D) 2,004

Fill in the correct circle.

Ⓐ   Ⓑ   Ⓒ   Ⓓ

Round down 2,379 to 2,000. Then round up 4,675 to 5,000. You can add 2,000 + 5,000 in your head. It's 7,000. Which answer comes closest? Estimating works well when you do not know the answer or you are trying to go faster on a test because time is short.

Now, what about recognizing a reasonable answer? Reasonable means "likely based on careful thinking." For instance, when you see the following problem, you know that 8,000 is clearly not a reasonable answer.

20
x 4

(A) 8,000
(B) 60
(C) 80
(D) 20

Fill in the correct circle.

Ⓐ   Ⓑ   Ⓒ   Ⓓ

Think it through: four 20s would never total 8,000! Also, multiplying 20 by 4 could not result in 20 again—that is not a reasonable answer either. You know these things already. Recognizing a reasonable answer is a powerful strategy when you want to eliminate answers. In other words, you can drop some answer choices immediately because they are not reasonable. Don't bother with answer choices that are clearly wrong because they are unreasonable. This improves your chances of choosing the correct answer, even if you have difficulty doing the problem.

Problem-Solving Test I

Directions: Solve each problem. Writr each answer in the space provided.

1. Max goes to the store to buy some school supplies. He buys two pencils at 29¢ each, a notebook that costs $1.19, and three folders that cost 39¢ each. (Prices include tax.) He pays with a $5.00 bill. How much change should he receive?

_____

2. A sixth grade class is going to the local library on a field trip. There are 24 students in the class. The teacher and seven parents will be driving the students in their cars. Each driver takes an equal amount of students. How many students are in each car?

_____

3. The students at Weller Elementary School are having a sale to earn money for their school. They are selling items they have made every day after school. The graph shows how much money they collected from their sale. How much money did the students collect for the whole week?

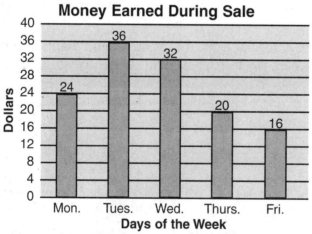

4. The sixth graders at Barnette Elementary School are taking a field trip to the zoo. Groups of at least 60 get a reduced rate on admission. The following classes are going:

Mr. Marchese	22
Mr. Shaw	26
Mrs. McLaughlin	24

Show how they could use front-end estimation to decide if they have enough students to get the reduced rate.

_____

_____

_____

_____

Problem-Solving Test I *(cont.)*

5. On June 6th, four girls go to the skating rink. Each girl has $10 to spend. They leave for the skating rink at 3:00 P.M. and return home at 8:00 P.M. How much money did they have to spend in all?

_____

6. Make the greatest sum possible with these digits: 4, 9, 6, and 7. Put each of these digits in one of the boxes below to make 2 two-digit numbers.

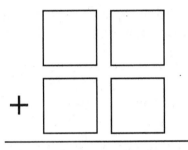

_____

7. Patty wants to build a fence around her garden. She wants the fenced area to be four feet by eight feet. How many feet of fencing does she need to go all around her garden?

8. Kyle and A. J. are playing a game. When Kyle says a number, A. J. does something to the number to get a different number. Look at the numbers they said:

Kyle	A. J.
24	6
16	4
32	8
8	2

_____

What number did A. J. say if Kyle said the number 36? Explain how you arrived at your answer.

_____

_____

_____

_____

Problem-Solving Test 1 *(cont.)*

9. It took Gwen and Kyleah 45 minutes to clean the basement. If they started at 3:45 P.M. and worked without stopping, what time was it when they were finished cleaning the basement?

_____

10. Riley had 36 cookies. He divided the cookies evenly into three boxes. Then he gave one of the boxes to a neighbor. How many cookies did he have left?

_____

11. Emily and Lisa had 10 pencils each. Nick had five pencils. Kitty had seven pencils. They put all the pencils in a big pile. Then they divided them into equal piles and each one took a pile. How many pencils did each one get?

_____

12. The first TV was invented in 1923. The first VCR was invented 46 years later. The first video game was invented three years after the VCR was invented. In what year were the VCR and the video game invented?

_____

Problem-Solving Test II

Directions: Use the information on the bar graph to solve the problems below.

The graph shown here illustrates how many pennies dated in the 1990s a child found. The years from 1990 to 1999 are written along the bottom. The number of pennies is written along the side. Each graph line increases by two.

1. Find the bar illustrating 1995. How many pennies were found with the 1995 date?

   _____

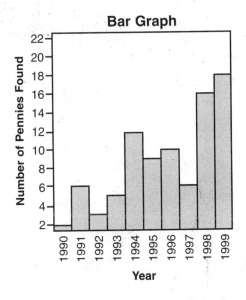

2. Find the bar showing 1992. Notice that the bar goes halfway between 2 and 4 on the left side. How many 1992 dates were found? _____

3. How many 1998 dates were found? _____

4. How many 1990 dates were found? _____

5. How many more pennies were found with 1999 dates than pennies with 1990 dates?

   _____

6. For which 2 years were the same number of pennies found? _____

7. What was the total number of pennies found for 1998 and 1999 dates? _____

8. Which 3 years had the fewest number of pennies? _____

9. Which 3 years had the most pennies? _____

10. What is the total number of pennies used in this data survey shown on the graph?

    _____

Problem-Solving Test II *(cont.)*

Directions: Use the information on the line graph below to solve the following problems.

The line graph shown here illustrates the number of drops of water children could put on a penny with an eye dropper before the bubble of water spilled off the penny. The names of each child are written on the graph lines along the base of the graph. The number of drops from 20 to 72 are recorded along the left side on the graph lines. The numbers increase by four from line to line.

11. Find Jenny's name along the bottom of the graph. Find the dot above her name. How many drops of water did she place on the penny before it spilled?

   _____

12. How many drops did Brian place on the penny? _____

13. How many drops did Julie place on the penny? _____

14. Mary's dot is halfway between the 52 and 56. How many drops did she place on the penny? _____

15. Which two children placed exactly the same number of drops on the penny?

   _____ _____

   How many drops did they each place on the penny? _____

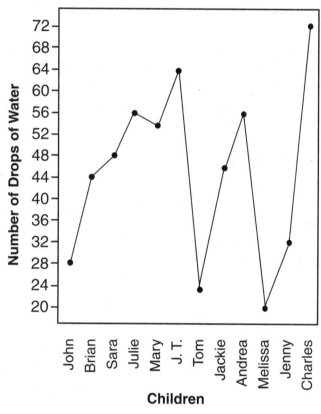

16. Who placed the fewest number of drops on the penny? _____

17. How many more drops did Charles place than Jenny? _____

18. How many more drops did J.T. place than Sara? _____

19. How many drops did J.T. and Charles together place ? _____

20. What was the total number of drops all of the students placed on the pennies?

   _____

Problem-Solving Test III

Directions: Use the circle graph to solve these word problems about ice cream flavors and restaurant favorites.

Favorite Ice Cream Flavors

This pie chart or circle graph shows the results of a survey of 100 third and fourth graders about their favorite types of ice cream.

1. Which ice cream flavor was the most popular?
   _____

2. Which ice cream flavors were the least popular?
   _____   _____

3. Which 2 flavors were equally popular?
   _____   _____

4. Which flavor was two times as popular as chocolate chip? _____

5. Which flavor was eight times as popular as butter pecan? _____

6. Which two flavors together were equal in popularity with the all-others category?
   _____   _____

Ice Cream Preferences

10% strawberry

15% chocolate

25% all others

5% butter pecan

5% chocolate chip

40% vanilla

Directions: Use the bar graph to answer each question.

7. About how much does it cost to see a play? _____

8. Which activity is the most expensive? _____

9. Which activity is the least expensive? _____

10. Which activity costs less, a concert or a dance? _____

11. About how much more does it cost to go to a dance than to a concert? _____

12. If you saw a play, a movie, a concert, and a dance in one month, about how much money would you spend? _____

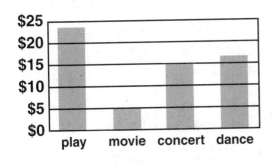

Cost of Entertainment

$25
$20
$15
$10
$5
$0
play   movie   concert   dance

Problem-Solving Test III *(cont.)*

Directions: Use the graph to answer each set of questions.

Television Viewing Hours of 5ᵗʰ and 6ᵗʰ Graders

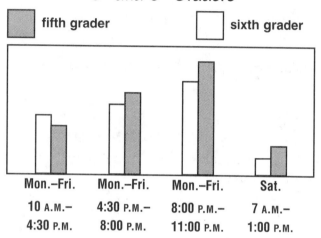

▨ fifth grader   ☐ sixth grader

Mon.–Fri. 10 A.M.–4:30 P.M.
Mon.–Fri. 4:30 P.M.–8:00 P.M.
Mon.–Fri. 8:00 P.M.–11:00 P.M.
Sat. 7 A.M.–1:00 P.M.

13. Do more fifth graders or sixth graders watch television on Saturday from 7 A.M. to 1 P.M.? _____

14. During which time period do fifth and sixth graders watch the greatest amount of television? _____

15. During which time period do fifth and sixth graders watch the least amount of television? _____

This shows the number of drinks served in one day.

Grissom Cafeteria Drinks

Drink	Number of Glasses
white milk	☐ ☐ ☐ ☐ ☐
chocolate milk	☐ ☐ ⌞
orange juice	☐ ☐
apple juice	☐ ⌞

☐ = 100 glasses   ⌞ = 50 glasses

16. How many glasses of white milk did the cafeteria serve? _____

17. How many glasses of orange and apple juice were served? _____

18. How many more glasses of orange juice than apple juice were served? _____

19. How many glasses of drinks were served in one day? _____

Animals in the Local Neighborhood

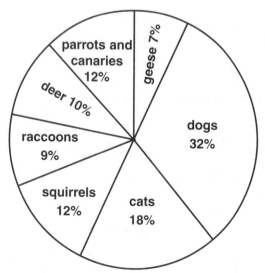

parrots and canaries 12%
geese 7%
deer 10%
raccoons 9%
squirrels 12%
cats 18%
dogs 32%

20. What percent of animals have wings? _____

21. What percent are house pets? _____

22. What percent have four legs? _____

23. What are the two most common wild animals in the neighborhood? _____

_____

24. If you add the squirrels, the deer, and the different types of birds together, are there more or fewer of them than dogs? _____

Problem Solving Test IV

Directions: Solve each problem and fill in the correct circle on the answer sheet on page 85.

1. There are eight bicycles. Half of them need to be fixed. How many need to be fixed? Fill in the circle next to your answer.

   Ⓐ 6   Ⓑ 4   Ⓒ 3

2. There are four pairs of children. Half of the children are going on a field trip. How many children are going on a field trip?

   Ⓐ 8   Ⓑ 2   Ⓒ 4

3. There are four sandwiches and six plates. If the sandwiches are cut in half and each half is put on a plate, how many sandwich halves will be left over?

   Ⓐ 4   Ⓑ 5   Ⓒ 2

donut	50¢	muffin	90¢
orange juice	75¢	milk	60¢
bagel	$1.00		

4. Marsha bought a muffin and milk. She paid $2.00. How much is her change?

   Ⓐ 75¢   Ⓑ 50¢   Ⓒ 55¢

5. Andrew bought a donut, orange juice, and a bagel. How much does he owe?

   Ⓐ $2.25   Ⓑ $2.00   Ⓒ $2.05

6. Kyle bought orange juice and paid $1.00. How much is his change?

   Ⓐ 50¢   Ⓑ 30¢   Ⓒ 25¢

7. Arthur bought a bagel and a milk. He paid $2.00. How much is his change?

   Ⓐ 40¢   Ⓑ 5¢   Ⓒ 25¢

8. Mr. Anderson bought three bagels. He paid $5.00. What is his change?

   Ⓐ $3.00   Ⓑ $1.00   Ⓒ $2.00

Problem-Solving Test IV *(cont.)*

9. Which is four dollars and twenty-seven cents?

   Ⓐ $40.27   Ⓒ $400.27

   Ⓑ $427   Ⓓ $4.27

10. How do you write $3.12?

    Ⓐ three twelve

    Ⓑ three dollars and twelve cents

    Ⓒ three point twelve cents

    Ⓓ dollars three and twelve

11. Mark cuts the grass for eight dollars an hour. He worked from two o'clock to five o'clock. How much did he earn?

    Ⓐ $34.00   Ⓒ $24.00

    Ⓑ $22.00   Ⓓ $27.00

12. Lupita babysits for 10 dollars an hour. She babysat from 6:00 to 8:30. How much did she earn?

    Ⓐ $40.00   Ⓒ $28.00

    Ⓑ $15.00   Ⓓ $25.00

13. Which group is closest in amount to one dollar?

    Ⓐ

    Ⓑ

    Ⓒ

    Ⓓ

14. Libbie's bed is four feet wide. About how many yards is that?

    Ⓐ four

    Ⓑ one yard and one foot

    Ⓒ two

    Ⓓ one yard and three feet

15. Angela bought a candy bar at the movies. She gave the boy at the counter four quarters. He gave her two dimes back. How much did the candy bar cost?

    Ⓐ $75   Ⓒ $1.20

    Ⓑ $.80   Ⓓ $.64

16. If July 4th is on a Wednesday, what day of the week will July 11th be?

    Ⓐ Tuesday   Ⓒ Monday

    Ⓑ Wednesday Ⓓ Thursday

17. Lupe and Kelly each decorated 6 eggs. They want to display them together. Which container will hold all of their eggs? Fill in the circle next to your answer.

    Ⓐ   Ⓑ

    Ⓒ    Ⓓ

18. Lauren read five books. Andrew read five books. Spencer read three books. How could you show this as a number sentence?

    Ⓐ 5 + 2 + 3   Ⓑ 5 x 2 + 3

    Ⓒ 5 x 5 + 3   Ⓓ 5 + 1 x 3

Problem-Solving Test IV (cont.)

Answer Sheet

1. Ⓐ Ⓑ Ⓒ
2. Ⓐ Ⓑ Ⓒ
3. Ⓐ Ⓑ Ⓒ
4. Ⓐ Ⓑ Ⓒ
5. Ⓐ Ⓑ Ⓒ
6. Ⓐ Ⓑ Ⓒ
7. Ⓐ Ⓑ Ⓒ
8. Ⓐ Ⓑ Ⓒ
9. Ⓐ Ⓑ Ⓒ Ⓓ
10. Ⓐ Ⓑ Ⓒ Ⓓ
11. Ⓐ Ⓑ Ⓒ Ⓓ
12. Ⓐ Ⓑ Ⓒ Ⓓ
13. Ⓐ Ⓑ Ⓒ Ⓓ
14. Ⓐ Ⓑ Ⓒ Ⓓ
15. Ⓐ Ⓑ Ⓒ Ⓓ
16. Ⓐ Ⓑ Ⓒ Ⓓ
17. Ⓐ Ⓑ Ⓒ Ⓓ
18. Ⓐ Ⓑ Ⓒ Ⓓ

Work Space

Problem-Solving Test V

Directions: Mark the space for the correct answer to each problem on the answer sheet given on page 89. Choose "none of these" if the right answer is not given.

1. At a football game, 1,364 people sat in the grandstands. Two hundred more stood by the fence and watched. How many saw the game?

   (A) 1,564   (D) 1,500

   (B) 1,164   (E) none of these

   (C) 1,664

2. Four girls in two houses are each six years old. How do you show this as a multiplication problem that equals 24 years?

   (A) 2 x 4   (D) 8 x 6

   (B) 2 x 4 x 6   (E) none of these

   (C) 4 x 6

3. There are only 101 chairs set up in the gym for the play. Three times that many are needed for the audience. How many are needed?

   (A) 301   (D) 104

   (B) 333   (E) none of these

   (C) 303

4. The newspaper said about 500 people attended a horse show. The newspaper was rounding to the nearest ten so about how many people attended the horse show?

   (A) 550   (D) 513

   (B) 496   (E) none of these

   (C) 489

5. You have two pies cut into eight pieces each. You put three pieces of one and two pieces of the other on a plate. What fraction of a pie do you have now?

   (A) 1/2   (D) eighths

   (B) 3/8   (E) none of these

   (C) 6/8

6. Dustin ran half of a mile in gym class in 129.6 seconds. If he ran one mile at the same speed, how many seconds would it take?

   (A) 300.9   (D) 259.2

   (B) 258.9   (E) none of these

   (C) 250.9

7. If you had $11.33 saved for a present that cost $18.80, how much more money would you need?

   (A) $9.47   (D) $7.53

   (B) $7.47   (E) none of these

   (C) $18.80

8. A square is cut into four equal pieces. One piece is taken away. What fraction of the square is left?

   (A) 3   (D) 1/2

   (B) 4/1   (E) none of these

   (C) 1/4

Problem-Solving Test V *(cont.)*

9. It takes 2 1/2 minutes to make a chocolate milkshake. Three children order milkshakes. How long will it take to make them?

   (A) 10 minutes   (D) 25 1/2 minutes

   (B) 12 1/2 minutes   (E) none of these

   (C) 8 1/2 minutes

10. A box of butter has four quarter-pound sticks of butter in it. How much does a box of butter weigh?

   (A) 4 lbs.   (D) 1/4 lb.

   (B) 1 lbs   (E) none of these

   (C) 1/2 lb.

Mrs. Ramirez, a fourth-grade teacher, will show a video for 30 minutes. If it is longer than that, she will continue it the next day.

Video Running Times	
Rip Van Winkle	90 minutes
Jumpin' Sam Patch	20 minutes
Pueblo Days	30 minutes
How Chicks Hatch	40 minutes

11. How many days will it take Mrs. Ramirez to show *Rip Van Winkle*?

   (A) 2.7 days   (D) 120 Minutes

   (B) 3 days   (E) none of these

   (C) 2 days

12. Which video could she show in less than one day?

   (A) *How Chicks Hatch*

   (B) *Pueblo Days*

   (C) *Rip Van Winkle*

   (D) *Jumpin' Sam Patch*

   (E) none of these

13. Which two videos would come out to two 30-minute showings exactly?

   (A) *How Chicks Hatch* and *Pueblo Days*

   (B) *Jumpin' Sam Patch* and *How Chicks Hatch*

   (C) *Jumpin' Sam Patch* and *Pueblo Days*

   (D) *Rip Van Winkle*

   (E) none of these

14. In a dart-throwing game, Darnell threw eight times and hit the target every fourth time. How many times did he hit the target?

   (A) 6   (D) 12

   (B) 8   (E) none of these

   (C) 3

15. Andre has set a reading goal. He's going to read two books every week for a month. How many books will he read in two months?

   (A) 16   (D) 30

   (B) 4   (E) none of these

   (C) 64

16. Tran has five adventure game CDs in his collection. His cousin is one year older than he is and has twice as many. How would you show the problem for how many CDs Tran's cousin has?

   (A) 5 x 2 + 1   (D) 5 + 1 x 2

   (B) 6 x 2   (E) none of these

   (C) 1 + 3 + 5

Problem-Solving Test V *(cont.)*

17. Berneitha, Karen, and Tamika went trick-or-treating on Halloween. Berneitha got seven pieces of gum; Karen got three; and Tamika got two. What was the average number of pieces of gum the girls received?

    (A) 3   (D) 12

    (B) 4   (E) none of these

    (C) 6

18. For the food drive at school, 16 students are each bringing seven cans. How many cans will they bring?

    (A) 23   (D) 118

    (B) 112   (E) none of these

    (C) 122

19. There are 30 children in gym class. Every fifth child is going to be a team leader. If the first team leader is child number 5 and the second team leader is child number 10, what number will the fourth team leader be?

    (A) 15   (D) 30

    (B) 25   (E) none of these

    (C) 20

20. Regina read 55 pages in the book. Norman read four times as many pages than Regina. How many pages did Norman read?

    (A) 200   (D) 260

    (B) 220   (E) none of these

    (C) 240

21. In four months, Margaret's brother Tim will be one year old. How old is Tim now?

    (A) five months   (D) eight months

    (B) seven months   (E) none of these

    (C) six months

22. Ron wants to make a special kind of punch that needs 1/2 gallon of ginger ale. He has a quart of ginger ale in the refrigerator. How much more does he need?

    (A) 3 quarts   (D) 2 cups

    (B) 2 quarts   (E) none of these

    (C) 1 quart

Trains to University Park		
Name	**Leaves**	**Arrives**
Flyer	5:02 P.M.	5:40 P.M.
Red Line	5:30 P.M.	6:10 P.M.
Sunset	5:45 P.M. (makes one stop)	6:30 P.M.

23. How long does the Flyer take to get to University Park?

    (A) 38 minutes   (D) 36 minutes

    (B) 1 hour, 2 minutes (E) none of these

    (C) 42 minutes

24. How long does the Red Line take to get to University Park?

    (A) 40 minutes   (D) 1 hour, 10 minutes

    (B) 20 minutes   (E) none of these

    (C) 50 minutes

Problem-Solving Test V *(cont.)*

Answer Sheet

Work Space

1. Ⓐ Ⓑ Ⓒ Ⓓ Ⓔ
2. Ⓐ Ⓑ Ⓒ Ⓓ Ⓔ
3. Ⓐ Ⓑ Ⓒ Ⓓ Ⓔ
4. Ⓐ Ⓑ Ⓒ Ⓓ Ⓔ
5. Ⓐ Ⓑ Ⓒ Ⓓ Ⓔ
6. Ⓐ Ⓑ Ⓒ Ⓓ Ⓔ
7. Ⓐ Ⓑ Ⓒ Ⓓ Ⓔ
8. Ⓐ Ⓑ Ⓒ Ⓓ Ⓔ
9. Ⓐ Ⓑ Ⓒ Ⓓ Ⓔ
10. Ⓐ Ⓑ Ⓒ Ⓓ Ⓔ
11. Ⓐ Ⓑ Ⓒ Ⓓ Ⓔ
12. Ⓐ Ⓑ Ⓒ Ⓓ Ⓔ
13. Ⓐ Ⓑ Ⓒ Ⓓ Ⓔ
14. Ⓐ Ⓑ Ⓒ Ⓓ Ⓔ
15. Ⓐ Ⓑ Ⓒ Ⓓ Ⓔ
16. Ⓐ Ⓑ Ⓒ Ⓓ Ⓔ
17. Ⓐ Ⓑ Ⓒ Ⓓ Ⓔ
18. Ⓐ Ⓑ Ⓒ Ⓓ Ⓔ
19. Ⓐ Ⓑ Ⓒ Ⓓ Ⓔ
20. Ⓐ Ⓑ Ⓒ Ⓓ Ⓔ
21. Ⓐ Ⓑ Ⓒ Ⓓ Ⓔ
22. Ⓐ Ⓑ Ⓒ Ⓓ Ⓔ
23. Ⓐ Ⓑ Ⓒ Ⓓ Ⓔ
24. Ⓐ Ⓑ Ⓒ Ⓓ Ⓔ

Problem-Solving Test VI

Directions: Mark the space for the correct answer to each problem on the answer sheet given on page 93. Choose "none of these" if the right answer is not given.

1. It is about 214 miles to fly from Paris to London. It is about 26 times farther to fly from Paris to Los Angeles. About how many miles is it from Paris to Los Angeles?

   (A) 5,564   (D) 4,654

   (B) 5,654   (E) none of these

   (C) 5,465

2. Kate found eight quarters, 66 dimes, 17 nickels, and eight pennies in her coin purse. How much money did Kate find?

   (A) $9.35   (D) $9.55

   (B) $9.45   (E) none of these

   (C) $8.85

3. A kilogram is 1,000 grams. Marc picked 3,000 kilograms of blueberries at a farm in Michigan. His mom used 2,000 grams for muffins and pancakes. How many kilograms of blueberries are left over?

   (A) 2 kg   (D) 5 kg

   (B) 1/2 kg   (E) none of these

   (C) 1 kg

4. Grandpa Morgan's deck behind his house is 18 feet wide. How many yards wide is it?

   (A) 6 yd.   (D) 9 yd.

   (B) 3 yd.   (E) none of these

   (C) 15 yd.

5. A quart of milk is half empty. How many cups are left?

   (A) 3 cups   (D) 1 cups

   (B) 4 cups   (E) none of these

   (C) 7 cups

6. A spaghetti recipe calls for one pound of stewed tomatoes. Robby has a can of stewed tomatoes in the cupboard that is 32 oz. How many pounds is the can in the cupboard?

   (A) 4 lbs.   (D) 3 lbs.

   (B) 2 lbs.   (E) none of these

   (C) 1 lbs.

7. Andrew bowled two games, scoring 193 and 206. What must he bowl in the third game in order to average 200 for the three games?

   (A) 196   (D) 205

   (B) 201   (E) none of these

   (C) 199

8. Juan typed 45 math problems in nine minutes. How many problems did he type in one minute?

   (A) 15 problems   (D) 14 problems

   (B) 6 problems   (E) none of these

   (C) 54 problems

Problem-Solving Test VI (cont.)

9. Mr. Anders is a salesman. He drives a total of 140 miles Monday through Friday. How many miles does he drive each day?

   (A) 20   (D) 24

   (B) 28   (E) none of these

   (C) 26

10. Coach Smith is adding grandstands to the football field. He needs to seat 1,500 people. Each grandstand seats a maximum of 500. How many should he order?

    (A) 10   (D) 5

    (B) 30   (E) none of these

    (C) 3

11. Marc has 140 cards in his collection. Half of them are sports figures. Half of that number are musicians. How many are musicians?

    (A) 70   (D) 30

    (B) 45   (E) none of these

    (C) 35

12. In a sack of bird seed, the ratio of sunflower seeds to corn kernels is 250 to 1000. Write this ratio as a fraction in its simplest form.

    (A) 1/4   (D) 1/2

    (B) 1/8   (E) none of these

    (C) 250/1000

13. Charlie sold 36 tickets to the Thanksgiving Day dinner for his club. Dustin sold 30. What is the ratio of the number of tickets Charlie sold to the number of tickets Dustin sold?

    (A) 5/6   (D) 5/11

    (B) 6/5   (E) none of these

    (C) 11/5

14. Spencer drove his car to visit his friend. His friend lives in a nearby town 96 miles away. If it took him 2 hours to get to his friend's house, how fast was he driving?

    (A) 26 mph   (D) 35 mph

    (B) 60 mph   (E) none of these

    (C) 12 mph

15. Mrs. Mikes, who runs the James Hart School store, has 28 tablets of paper, 98 erasers, and 196 pencils. She wants to divide the supplies into groups so that each group has an equal number of tablets, an equal number of erasers, and an equal number of pencils. What is the maximum number of groups she can make?

    (A) 7   (D) 14

    (B) 2   (E) none of these

    (C) 28

16. Eli is trying to calculate how much he spent at the hardware store. He bought 50 bolts, 20 nuts, and 100 washers. Each bolt cost 35¢. A nut cost 25¢, and a washer cost 10¢. How much did he spend?

    (A) $22.50   (D) $20.55

    (B) $10.00   (E) none of these

    (C) $57.45

17. Diane is having a party. For a bowl of mixed nuts, she already used a 1/2 pound of peanuts, 1/2 pound of walnuts, 3/4 pound of raisins, and a 2/3 pound of pecans. If she wanted to double the recipe, how many more pounds of peanuts would she need to buy?

    (A) 1/2 pound   (D) 1/4 pound

    (B) 1 pound   (E) none of these

    (C) 1 1/2 pound

18. Bill, the janitor, glued two sheets of plywood together for strength. One sheet was 1/32 inch thick, and the other was 13/32 inch thick. How thick was the new board?

    (A) 7/32 inch   (D) 3/8 thick

    (B) 7/16 inch   (E) none of these

    (C) 13/1024 inch

19. Maggie is getting ready for the one-mile race in June. The first day of practice she ran 1/3 of a mile; the second day she ran 1/2 mile; and the third day she ran 5/8 of a mile. Which is closest to her total mileage for the three days?

    (A) 1 1/4 miles   (D) 1 3/4 miles

    (B) 1 1/2 miles   (E) none of these

    (C) 1 1/8 miles

20. There are 20 people on your baseball team. One-fourth of the team was chosen to play on an all-star team at the end of the season. How many were chosen?

    (A) 10   (D) 5

    (B) 15   (E) none of these

    (C) 16

21. At a baseball game, 6,591 people sat in the grandstands. 125 more stood by the fence and watched. How many saw the game?

    (A) 6,716   (D) 1,500

    (B) 1,164   (E) none of these

    (C) 1,664

22. Fourteen girls in five classrooms are nine years old. How would you show this as a multiplication problem that equals 126 years?

    (A) 2 x 4   (D) 8 x 6

    (B) 2 x 4 x 6   (E) none of these

    (C) 14 x 9

23. There are only 214 chairs set up in the auditorium. Three times that many are needed for the audience. How many are needed?

    (A) 301   (D) 104

    (B) 333   (E) none of these

    (C) 642

24. Joe has 47 baseball cards. Jack has three times as many baseball cards as Joe. Danny has four fewer baseball cards than Jack. How many baseball cards does Danny have?

    (A) 141   (C) 189

    (B) 137   (E) none of these

    (C) 145

Problem-Solving Test VI *(cont.)*

Answer Sheet

1. Ⓐ Ⓑ Ⓒ Ⓓ Ⓔ
2. Ⓐ Ⓑ Ⓒ Ⓓ Ⓔ
3. Ⓐ Ⓑ Ⓒ Ⓓ Ⓔ
4. Ⓐ Ⓑ Ⓒ Ⓓ Ⓔ
5. Ⓐ Ⓑ Ⓒ Ⓓ Ⓔ
6. Ⓐ Ⓑ Ⓒ Ⓓ Ⓔ
7. Ⓐ Ⓑ Ⓒ Ⓓ Ⓔ
8. Ⓐ Ⓑ Ⓒ Ⓓ Ⓔ
9. Ⓐ Ⓑ Ⓒ Ⓓ Ⓔ
10. Ⓐ Ⓑ Ⓒ Ⓓ Ⓔ
11. Ⓐ Ⓑ Ⓒ Ⓓ Ⓔ
12. Ⓐ Ⓑ Ⓒ Ⓓ Ⓔ
13. Ⓐ Ⓑ Ⓒ Ⓓ Ⓔ
14. Ⓐ Ⓑ Ⓒ Ⓓ Ⓔ
15. Ⓐ Ⓑ Ⓒ Ⓓ Ⓔ
16. Ⓐ Ⓑ Ⓒ Ⓓ Ⓔ
17. Ⓐ Ⓑ Ⓒ Ⓓ Ⓔ
18. Ⓐ Ⓑ Ⓒ Ⓓ Ⓔ
19. Ⓐ Ⓑ Ⓒ Ⓓ Ⓔ
20. Ⓐ Ⓑ Ⓒ Ⓓ Ⓔ
21. Ⓐ Ⓑ Ⓒ Ⓓ Ⓔ
22. Ⓐ Ⓑ Ⓒ Ⓓ Ⓔ
23. Ⓐ Ⓑ Ⓒ Ⓓ Ⓔ
24. Ⓐ Ⓑ Ⓒ Ⓓ Ⓔ

Work Space

Answer Key

Page 8
1. 110 baseballs
2. 369 baseball cards

Page 9
1. Nile River is 6,671 km long. Mississippi River is 5,971 km long.
2. She spends $14.77. She receives $5.23 in change.

Page 10
1. 32 cookies left
2. 5 cookies each

Page 11
1. $6.70
2. 5 cars

Page 12
1. You are more likely to pull out an unsharpened pencil because there are almost twice as many unsharpened pencils as sharpened pencils in the bag.
2. 250 people

Page 13
1. $8.84
2. 80 + 80 + 70 + 60 + 70 = 360

Page 14
1. 13 teams
2. B

Page 15
1. They are polygons. They are closed figures.
2. 35 + 29 = 64 or 25 + 39 = 64

Page 16
1. 20. Whenever Jill said a number, Bob divided it by 5 to get his number. Since Bob said 4, then Jill must have said 20. 20 ÷ 5 = 4.
2. $15

Page 17
1. 3 pennies, 3 dimes, 1 nickel
2. 6 cows, 5 chickens

Page 19
1. $7.00 is his change.
2. 32 feet of fencing

Page 20
1. 39
2. $525

Page 21
1. 6:25 P.M.
2. $75

Page 22
1. $16
2. 48 inches, $2.40

Page 23
1. 30 + 80 + 30 = 140
2. B (because the three dominoes on top have 7 dots on them and "B" is the only one of the choices that has 7 dots.)

Page 24
1. 74 + 85 = 159 or 84 + 75 = 159
2. 40

Page 25
1. Multiply by 3 and add 1.
2. There are more chances of getting a butterscotch from the blue bag because even though there are fewer pieces than in the red bag, more of the total pieces are butterscotch.

Page 26
1. $100
2. 9 parents

Page 27
1. 5
2. 17 boys and 13 girls

Page 28
1. $148
2. $50

Pages 30 and 31
1. 119 video games
2. $6.75
3. The Asian elephant's life span is 40 years, and the box turtle's life span is 100 years.
4. $3.00
5. 24 cookies
6. 6 cookies

Pages 32 and 33
1. 3 inches
2. $7.50
3. 4 boxes
4. $5.50
5. Eric has 9, Jeff has 15, Zach has 10, and Josh has 14.
6. 6 inches

Pages 34 and 35
1. 5 feet
2. 3 boxes; 3 boxes
3. 4 inches
4. $7.00
5. 5 points
6. 2 boxes

Pages 36 and 37
1. 800
2. 200
3. 50
4. 9:30 P.M.
5. 120 lb.
6. 16 ft.

Pages 38 and 39
1. 12 fish
2. 1,136 miles
3. Some possible answers: 5 dimes, 1 nickel, 4 pennies or 1 quarter, 3 dimes, 4 pennies
4. $90
5. Her items cost $6.71. Her change would be $3.29
6. 10 cm

Pages 40 and 41
1. $40
2. 762 miles
3. Some possible answers: 3 quarters, 2 pennies or 2 quarters, 2 dimes, 1 nickel, 2 pennies or 7 dimes, 1 nickel, 2 pennies
4. 12¢
5. You are more likely to get a 6, 7, or 8 than a 2 or a 12 because there are several ways you can get 6, 7, or 8. There is only one way to get a 2 or a 12.

Answer Key *(cont.)*

Pages 42 and 43

1. The game is not fair. The friend is more likely to win because there is more area on the spinner covered with odd numbers than even numbers.
2. Each person would get 3 cookies.
3. $2.84
4. 25¢
5. 80 feet

Pages 44 and 45

1. You are more likely to pick a gray marble from the brown bag because there are more gray marbles than black marbles in that bag than there are in the white bag.
2. $2.00 + $3.00 + $8.00 + $1.00 = $14.00, $20.00 − $14.00 = $6.00
3. 84 + 72 = 156 or 82 + 74 = 156
4. 50 minutes
5. 22 feet, $44.00

Pages 46 and 47

1. $8
2. 2:25 P.M.
3. 18 squares
4. $315
5. 36¢
6. Store C. The pencils at Store A cost 10¢ each, the pencils at Store B cost 9¢ each, and the pencils at Store C cost only 8¢ each.

Pages 48 and 49

1. Mara's birthday is Sept. 8th. Sherry's birthday is Sept. 17th.
2. Natalie, Noriko, Leo (or) Leo, Noriko, Natalie
3. Jessica and Mrs. Connor
4. town hall, library, bank, post office
5. Robin
6. Lynette; Daryl
7. Nicholas; Daryl
8. Nicholas; Daryl
9. Robin; Tyler
10. Nicholas
11. Maya and Lisa

12. Mark, Daryl, Tyler, Maria, Lynette, Lance, Robin, Nicholas

Pages 52 and 53

1. $7.50
2. 7:20 A.M.
3. The books cost a total of $9.80. He receives $10.20 in change.
4. 4 boxes
5. 16 feet
6. 2 boxes

Pages 54 and 55

1. $24
2. Ben has enough money because $1.00 + $3.00 + $2.00 = $6.00; yes
3. 2 pizzas
4. $104
5. 30 prizes

Pages 56 and 57

1. $360
2. 20 times
3. The items cost $8.75. Her change would be $11.25.
4. Jason ate more of his pizza because Jason cut his pizza into only 6 pieces so his pieces were bigger than Aaron's.
5. Shannon can purchase a hair accessory, journal, and magnet for $9.23 and receive $0.77 in change.

Pages 58 and 59

1. 48 quarters
2. 420 times
3. $2.80
4. 40
5. Her change was $4.33.
6. Five packs of gum at 35¢ each are a better deal because 5 packs for $1.90 means each pack costs 38¢.

Pages 60 and 61

1. $12.50
2. 54 cakes
3. 1 hour and 24 minutes
4. The diameter of Earth is 7,926 miles. The diameter of Mercury is 3,032 miles.

5. $30.36
6. 2 cookies

Pages 62 and 63

1. 12 pieces of candy each
2. $87.00
3. 7 cm
4. You are more likely to pull out a white marble since there are more white marbles in the bag than blue marbles.
5. 4 students per car

Pages 64 and 65

1. You need to know how many hours she worked each week.
2. They are polygons.
3. 2 feet
4. 17 + 48 = 65 or 18 + 47 = 65
5. Anne said the number 30, because each time Anne multiplied the number Ellen said by 5.

Pages 66 and 67

1. She would need 7 boxes. They would cost $27.93.
2. His change is $10.51.
3. 90¢
4. 8 students
5. Store C. Notebooks at Store A cost $1.33 each. Notebooks at Store B cost $1.49. Notebooks at Store C cost $1.29 each.

Pages 68 and 69

1. 3 packages
2. The fourth graders ate 24 pizzas.
3. $5.64
4. You need to know how many of each type of gift wrap they sold.
5. 6 inches by 12 inches

Answer Key (cont.)

Pages 70–72

1. 38 hours; $266
2. b; $58
3. d; 360 lbs.
4. 10 P.M. is 9 hours later. If the clock loses 3 minutes every hour, it will be 27 minutes behind or 9:33 P.M. when it is supposed to read 10 P.M.
5. number of houses = $4,608/$256 per house = 18 houses
6. $0.23 is spent on the peel; $1.80 – $0.23 = $1.57 on the banana
7. James spent $37.43; he saved $12.47
8. Laurel paid $13.50 for the gift. Joey paid $9.00 for the gift.
9. $10.31
10. $30.05
11. 36,809.6 miles
12. 30 pieces of candy
13. 14 hours and 40 minutes
14. 144 pens
15. 9 students

Pages 76–78

1. His change is $2.06
2. 3 students in each car
3. $128
4. 20 + 30 + 20 = 70
5. $40
6. 94 + 76 = 170 or 96 + 74 = 170
7. 24 feet
8. A. J. said the number 9 because every time Kyle said a number, A. J. divided the number Kyle said by 4.
9. 4:30 P.M.
10. 24 cookies were left.
11. They each got 8 pencils.
12. The VCR was invented in 1969. The video game was invented in 1972.

Pages 79 and 80

1. 9 pennies
2. 3
3. 16
4. 2

5. 16 pennies
6. 1991 and 1997
7. 34 pennies
8. 1990, 1992, 1993
9. 1994, 1998, 1999
10. 87 pennies
11. 32 drops
12. 44 drops
13. 56 drops
14. 54 drops
15. Julie, Andrea; 56 drops
16. Melissa
17. 40 drops
18. 16 drops
19. 136 drops
20. 544 drops

Pages 81 and 82

1. vanilla
2. butter pecan and chocolate chip
3. butter pecan and chocolate chip
4. strawberry
5. vanilla
6. chocolate and strawberry
7. $24
8. play
9. movie
10. concert
11. $2
12. $60
13. fifth graders
14. Mon.–Fri., 8–11 P.M.
15. Sat., 7 A.M.– 1 P.M.
16. 500 glasses
17. 350 glasses
18. 50 glasses
19. 1,100 glasses
20. 19%
21. 50%
22. 81%
23. deer and squirrels
24. more

Pages 83 and 84

1. B
2. C
3. C
4. B
5. A
6. C
7. A
8. C
9. D
10. B
11. C
12. D
13. B
14. B
15. B
16. B
17. D
18. B

Pages 86–88

1. A
2. C
3. C
4. B
5. E
6. D
7. B
8. E
9. E
10. B
11. B
12. D
13. B
14. E
15. A
16. E
17. B
18. E
19. C
20. B
21. D
22. C
23. A
24. A

Pages 90–92

1. A
2. E
3. C
4. A
5. E
6. B
7. B
8. E
9. B
10. C
11. C
12. A
13. B
14. E
15. D
16. E
17. A
18. B
19. B
20. D
21. A
22. C
23. C
24. B